AMONG RUINS

THE ERNEST SANDEEN PRIZE IN POETRY

Editors
Joyelle McSweeney, Orlando Menes

2017	*Among Ruins*, Robert Gibb
2015	*Underdays*, Martin Ott
2013	*The Yearning Feed*, Manuel Paul López
2011	*Dreamlife of a Philanthropist*, Janet Kaplan
2009	*Juan Luna's Revolver*, Louisa A. Igloria

Editor
John Matthias (1997–2007)

2007	*The Curator of Silence*, Jude Nutter
2005	*Lives of the Sleepers*, Ned Balbo
2003	*Breeze*, John Latta
2001	*No Messages*, Robert Hahn
1999	*The Green Tuxedo*, Janet Holmes
1997	*True North*, Stephanie Strickland

ROBERT GIBB

AMONG RUINS

University of Notre Dame Press
Notre Dame, Indiana

Copyright © 2017 by Robert Gibb

Published by the University of Notre Dame Press
Notre Dame, Indiana 46556 USA
undpress.nd.edu

All Rights Reserved

Library of Congress Cataloging-in-Publication Data

Names: Gibb, Robert, 1946– author.
Title: Among ruins / Robert Gibb.
Description: Notre Dame, Indiana : University of Notre Dame Press, [2017] |
 Series: The Ernest Sandeen Prize in Poetry |
Identifiers: LCCN 2017025415 (print) | LCCN 2017025445 (ebook) | ISBN
 9780268102111 (pdf) | ISBN 9780268102128 (epub) | ISBN 9780268102098
 (hardback) | ISBN 0268102090 (hardcover) | ISBN 9780268102104 (paper)
Subjects: | BISAC: POETRY / American / General. | LITERARY CRITICISM /
 Poetry. | POETRY / General.
Classification: LCC PS3557.I139 (ebook) | LCC PS3557.I139 A6 2017 (print) |
 DDC 811/.54—dc23
LC record available at https://lccn.loc.gov/2017025415

∞*This paper meets the requirements of ANSI/NISO Z39.48-1992
(Permanence of Paper).*

for Maggie

CONTENTS

Acknowledgments	xi
Pittsburgh Memories (1984)	1

I

On Douglas Cooper's *University Center Mural* (1995–1996), Carnegie Mellon University	4
Two Views of the River	6
Swimming at Night	8
100-Inch Mill, Special Plate Finishing Facility	10
Pittsburgh Photographs	12
Light Rail	13
Half-Light	
1. *Driving Home from the Post Office*	14
2. *"Group Finds Homestead Police Station Is Haunted"*	15
3. *A Brief History of Photography*	17
4. *Time Exposure*	19
Driving Back to Homestead Park after an Absence of Almost 30 Years	20

II

The Committee on Uniform Nomenclature	24
The Gorsons in the Spanierman Gallery	25

Insomnia	27
Moby-Dick	28
Among Ruins	
1. *Smokestack, 160-Inch Mill*	29
2. *Words Written for the Historical Marker Planned for the 12,000-Ton Press*	31
The Book of Generations Tucked among the Pages of the Family Bible	32
The Negro Leagues	
1. *At the Renaming Ceremony*	34
2. *Keeping Score*	36
3. *"The Homestead Grays"*	37
Donny	38
W. Eugene Smith: Three Photographs	40

III

"Beauties of the Common Tool"	44
Industrial Pittsburgh: Works on Paper	45
Dreiser First Glimpses *Sister Carrie* in the Stacks of the Carnegie Library	47
Making Pittsburgh Stogies	49
Ahmad Jamal Playing the Piano at the Kay Boys' Club, ca. 1945	50
The Piano	52
Jobs Report	54
The Dinner Pail	57
Historical Portraits	
1. *John McClure*	59
2. *Philander C. Knox*	60
Newspaper Days: Dreiser in Pittsburgh, 1893–1894	61

IV

Looking through the Entries in an Old Pocket Notebook	66
Children Going Home from School to New Raw Suburbs (1952): Photograph by Clyde Hare	67
Childhood	69
Double Shot	70
View of Toledo	72
Lunar Grammars	74
On Foot	76
The Art of Memory	78
Envoy: *University Center Mural* (1995–1996), Carnegie Mellon University	80
Notes	81

ACKNOWLEDGMENTS

Grateful acknowledgment is made to the following journals in which earlier versions of these poems first appeared:

Aethlon: "The Homestead Grays"
Arts & Letters: "Childhood," "*Children Going Home from School to New Raw Suburbs* (1952): Photograph by Clyde Hare"
Battistrada Arts Review: "Dreiser First Glimpses *Sister Carrie* in the Stacks of the Carnegie Library," "Historical Portraits," "*Newspaper Days*: Dreiser in Pittsburgh, 1893–1894"
Brilliant Corners: "Ahmad Jamal Playing the Piano at the Kay Boys' Club, ca. 1945," "Double Shot," "The Piano," "*Pittsburgh Memories* (1984)"
Fourth River: "Envoy: *University Center Mural* (1995–1996), Carnegie Mellon University" (as "Taking One More Look at Pittsburgh in Douglas Cooper's Memory Mural")
The Gettysburg Review: "Industrial Pittsburgh: Works on Paper"
Great River Review: "The Art of Memory," "Light Rail," "Lunar Grammars"
The Hudson Review: "Among Ruins," "The Dinner Pail," "Two Views of the River"
Missouri Review: "Insomnia," "Swimming at Night"
New Letters: "100-Inch Mill, Special Plate Finishing Facility"
Notre Dame Review: "Donny," "The Gorsons in the Spanierman Gallery," "Half-Light," "*Moby-Dick*," "On Douglas Cooper's *University Center Mural* (1995–1996), Carnegie Mellon University," "On Foot," "Pittsburgh Photographs," "W. Eugene Smith: Three Photographs"
Pittsburgh Post-Gazette: "At the Renaming Ceremony," "The Committee on Uniform Nomenclature," "Keeping Score"

Poetry East: "'Beauties of the Common Tool,'" "The Book of Generations Tucked among the Pages of the Family Bible," "Driving Back to Homestead Park after an Absence of Almost 30 Years," "*Making Pittsburgh Stogies*"
Prairie Schooner: "*View of Toledo*"
Southern Review: "Looking through the Entries in an Old Pocket Notebook"

Part one of "Jobs Report" originally appeared in *Battistrada Arts Review,* part two in *West Branch.*

You wanted to paint Pittsburgh.
—Hayden Carruth

Pittsburgh Memories *(1984)*

Romare Bearden, 1911–1988

A world on which the curtain's gone up:
Silhouette faces,
Cut-and-paste,
The collage's quilt of colors—

Or "cutaway house," as the catalogue calls it,
Inside and out on view,
One window see-through
In the back, one up front blacked out.

The colors in the parlor are almost tropical
Where three people sit
As if for a group portrait,
One of the faces pure African mask,

Though actually this is Pittsburgh,
His grandmother's
Boardinghouse, steelworkers
To the rafters. "Look around that room,"

The catalogue suggests. "What do you see?"
(The dust broom on the floor,
The funnel horn
And turntable of an old Victrola.)

"Which forms look soft and blurry?
Which fracture space
So that it jubilates
 Like music from the Red Hot Peppers?"

Smoke above the mills and a chuffing train:
Outside it's factory time—
Flat paint, straight lines—
Weary blues kicking off each shift.

I

On Douglas Cooper's *University Center Mural* (1995–1996), Carnegie Mellon University

i.

Coming in again from the present
As if it were a kind of weather, I'm stunned
As always at the tonnage of the visual field
He's managed to array in place,
The great colonnades of the smokestacks
And silos of the blast furnace stoves
Rendered in charcoal because charcoal
Has burned, the rivers the paper's white fire.
All of it carbon and traces of ash,
Archival because sealed from the acids.

ii.

All of it parallax and skew, the hub
Of the rotunda crowded with rooftops,
Storefronts like postage stamps pasted in rows,
The graphic pattern of city blocks
Crisscrossed back to their vanishing points . . .
A Pittsburgh configured in the steel dust.
Or say the past here were *pentimento*
And presented before the fact—the world
That's come to pass leveraged upon it,
Cancelling kingdoms from the stamps.

iii.

The narrow houses, sun-half and shadow,
Winding like dominos up and down the hills,
And on the foreground ridge of porches
People sitting out, the industrial
Summer twilight spread about them.
Some of the neighborhoods recede in space,
Some are hung vertically like quilts.
Sightlines and time frames. The warp
Of the landscape into buckled wards,
Crammed into the wedge of the confluence.

iv.

East wall or west, figures in the pattern
Are templates, mapped across time,
The mural Mercator of panels
On which memory has prepared its ground.
Shops façaded under awnings and signs.
Streets you could walk through, after,
As though down into the past. For the students
It's pretty much that—black-and-white
And backdrop to the laptop world—
Though they pass from sight before it.

Two Views of the River

i.

The floating acres drifting slowly past:
Barges and the broad shoals of the river
On which the tug waves break, a stand
Of sandbar willows canted over water,

Their thin leaves flashing like riffles
Where the crucible mills poured fire,
Slag erupted nightly above the other shore.
Flowing north, the river here cuts west,

Beyond the trestle and Glenwood Bridge,
The color of whatever recent weather,
And disappears between the pitched banks
Which gave it its name—*Monongahela*—

Skyscrapers glinting in the distance,
And that lone gull stalled in the winds
It's been riding inland above the valley,
A consequence of the waters, as are we.

ii.

I paced out their width once, crossing
The bridge at the end of a summer day,
The home half of the river spreading away,
The railing's chipped Art Deco tulips

Marking my stride. If I looked up at the hill
On which I now stand looking down,
I'd have seen the last level rays of light
Molten among the deep-crowned trees,

And to my right the waters, pewter
To zinc to tungsten, flowing into the sun.
It seemed to take the whole late afternoon,
With supper waiting. In the dream

I have of hurrying home, alone—
The mills in shadow, the river giving back
The sky—the way is always over water
I'm never more than halfway across.

Swimming at Night

Warm nights we'd park the car there
Across the river where Saline Street stopped,
The boat ramp vanished into the black
Lapping oils at the shoreline.

Stripped clear to our skivvies,
We'd pick our way past beer cans
And wrappers, the odd condom floating
Like a small translucent fish,

And slip into that body of darkness
Which buoyed us up, out beneath
The High Level Bridge.
Fires from Mesta and United States Steel

Flickered among the neon on the river,
The constellations blazing above us—
A glittering cold city in the air.
Up to our necks, we'd churn in place,

Arms slowly wreathing the surface.
I'd like to swim out again, alone,
To the first stone abutment of the bridge,
In order to breaststroke back,

Watching as moonlight lustered
The shapes of girls who were changing
Into women before me.
I'd like to hear her tell me once more

That her nipples were just like mine,
And sink into that Egypt,
The barges beyond us freighting their coals,
The mills like burning foothills.

100-Inch Mill, Special Plate Finishing Facility

i.

All week it all keeps running through my head:
Lightnin' Hopkins, his fingerpicked riffs
And notes pulled off with the fretting hand,
His Piney Woods' vocals at the top of the mix—

Workin' in a steel mill . . . hand me down my pay.

In 1965, from the ground up, the mills are clamor,
So loud my ears ring for the first week I'm anywhere
But in them,
            the decibel levels you can hear
From miles away, hammering through the valley.

Inside, it's whistle and steam, the heavy metal riot
Of machinery, charged slabs rolled into plate.

It's "Moon Rise Blues" when you wake to work
At midnight, the conveyor belts sluicing steel.

Grab a pick and shovel and roll from sun to sun.

Because it's night we won't see those shafts of light
Streaming through the cracks in the roof, the cloudy
Windows where the brick-colored dust boils up.

This ruddled glow's cast from the ovens, ingots,
Sparks in a shower, slabs with their ratchel of scale.

ii.

All night in the great halls of the rolling mills
I'm abandoned to the slabs of the hours,
Haunted by snatches of the same stark song—

the moon is rising—one of his old Aladdin sides.

When I break for lunch, the moon's in the middle
Of the river, a wafer on the waters, coming apart.

All night I've been hosing out blasts of steam—
Cleaning oil spots and dribbled slicks
(Little wheels of iridescence) from the stacks
Of special plate the gantry crane keeps bringing—
Bursts of scalding mist
That could bubble skin right off the shins.

Name me the blues for that.

Lightnin' could, although he's worried mostly
About his woman and the fact that he *don't work
in no candy kitchen,* the flashing notes slashed out.

Steel strings, I remember thinking, steel wheels
On the rails he's riding home,
                              rollin' and rollin',
Blues in both the idiom and the mode.

Pittsburgh Photographs

Clyde Hare, 1927–2009

1. *"Last Steam Train," 1951*

A long white cumulus plume trailing beneath a hill
Whose blackness is blotter at this time of day,
Silhouetted houses above it crenellating the frame,
The train itself invisible and giving up the ghost.

2. *"Horse and Wagon on Smithfield Street Bridge," 1954*

Twilight and the bridge above the river faded in mist,
The world paraded in profile across it—commuter traffic
And a trolley and that remnant of the past, the gift
Of its animal transit, clattering beside the trolley tracks.

3. *"Early Fog on the Mon. Parked Cars and Towboat," 1957*

The shelf of wharf in the foreground glazed white
With an overnight snow, and those cars slotted head-on
To the river, the towboat and barge beyond them
Floating in fog as in the milk-jade clouds of heaven.

Light Rail

A trolley like a lantern hung by its handle,
With a stop at the top of my street.

Grooved tracks and, overhead, that grid
Of electric netting,

The skirts of the fenders in winter
Running just above the snow,

Though in any weather it was magic—
Clattering, loaf-shaped, amps of the carriage,

The man a conductor as well.

It took me down a hill I thought was north
And steep as the sides of the globe,

The trolley island below in Homestead
Wide as a sidewalk and half-a-block long.

"What would the world look like," Einstein
Wondered, "if I rode on a beam of light?"

Returning at night, I'd wait on that island
For the last fires of transit

To come shuttling down the wire.

Half-Light

1. *Driving Home from the Post Office*

Eighth and McClure, waiting for the light,
The thought comes out of nowhere—
I used to live here. I look down a block
Of Homestead from which Homestead is gone:
Grant's and Woolworth's and Thom McAn's,
All vanished. And Wolfson's bakery, where loaves
I watched judder through the slicer
Were miraculously snatched up whole.

Half Brothers is now a thrift shop,
Peter Pan Paint and Hardware
The local outlet of Saint Vincent de Paul.
And those hardwood lanes and gutters
In which the duckpins were scattered—
Where's Banquo when there's no banquet hall?

2. "Group Finds Homestead Police Station Is Haunted"

Members of the Greater Pittsburgh Paranormal Society
today showed Homestead police and borough staff video and
audio evidence.
>—*Pittsburgh Post-Gazette*

As if the building were some sort of palimpsest,
Which, being the old post office, it is,

Presences instead of ghostly script
Lurking among the surfaces.

Though that's hardly what *haunted* means
To either the paranormals or the police,

Under surveillance as they come and go,
Or so it seems, beneath that one side window.

And there in one of the videos a shadow
Can be seen shuttling through the room

In which my Uncle Arch worked at his desk,
Surrounded by ink pads and rubber stamps,

The small engraved emperies of postage—
All of it wonderful to me as the sealing wax

Kings in movies pressed their signet rings into.
As the rings I'd make of his cigar bands.

Sometimes, out playing, I'd stop by,
Waiting beneath the window to surprise him.

Nineteen fifty-something, one of the years
Before he died and something besides him

Was gone from the world forever.
Haunt, as in being present, continually in mind.

Or a shadow like the spirit passing,
Magnetic, on the bandwidths of the tape.

3. *A Brief History of Photography*

Making the shadows permanent was the first hurdle.
After that it was faces, mostly, and landscapes.
Then corpses from the war.

In Pittsburgh, where Carnegie was making a fortune
On armor plate and posing in a sash
For his photograph,

The fall of light on tin and glass and silver meant
One technology's attendance on another.
As did Dabbs's sequence

Documenting the Battle of Homestead (ca. 1892)
When the world in the form of barges
Was going up in smoke,

Billows blanketing the struck mills under attack.
By comparison, that boxed set of studies
Of the Westinghouse plant

In 1904 could be a poster for the industrial world
Such as management envisions it,
All tidy and secured.

Soon photos from inside the mills will start to appear,
Workers grouped among shafts of light
Cascading onto the shop floor,

Or isolated at their labors among the various sources
Of fire. Blast furnace and open hearth
So many candles to the lens.

Before long it will all seem generic, even the titles—
Worker Watching Ladle (1934)—of a piece
With its period,

The lunch pails and moustaches and newsboy caps,
And the way that each photo becomes, in time,
A present image of the past.

4. *Time Exposure*

What ever happened to those faces in the old photographs?
—John Stewart

They're ushering in the afterlife, I think again
This morning, marking the moment
They've been marked by.

In Johnstown, 1889, it's the aftermath of flood,
Buildings so much rubble, piled up
Like boxcars in a wreck,

The paused crews on the rooftops staring back
From what even then was *history*,
Come home to roost.

*

Perched, grave, archival, beached amid debris
In which they've yet to make a dent,
Ringed by standing water . . .

It's possible my own people are there among them,
Now grown anonymous, familiar only
The way faces are

When grouped by disaster, or simply singled out
From the lives they'll get back to,
Any moment now.

Driving Back to Homestead Park after an Absence of Almost 30 Years

January 1992

i.

Now then, the trestles hum, *now then,*
The whole potholed length of the bridge,
The ruins of the Industrial Revolution

Scuttled and rusting along the river below.
Now then, where the thin light of winter
Falls like snow upon the tiered avenues,

The cold sill of the ice house, emptied
Of its null gray blocks. Then past
The new wing of the hospital, decades old,

The close lawns and suburbs of the dead
Spreading along both sides of the road,
Gravestones heaved as cakes in a floe.

ii.

And now over another fold of landscape
Into Homestead Park, wondering
What's become of all the shade trees

That used to nave the summer streets,
Then down my own defoliate road
To park before the house I grew up in.

Engine idling, what should I remember
After all this time but the single die
I dropped through a knothole in the floor,

Wondering if it's still down there—
One half of a number which, now as then,
There is no way to add up again.

The Committee on Uniform Nomenclature

> The definition of steel is in a shockingly bad condition.
> —*Metallurgy of Iron and Steel* (1907)

They wanted a language standardized as Greenwich Time,
Plain direct terms defining the line between *cast iron*
And *wrought, pig iron* and *steel*, their allotments of carbon.

Terms as blunt and functional as the names for tools.
Shaped verbatim to freight on the tongue. When annealed,
All iron becomes malleable and converts to grades of steel.

You worked your way among them, grown fluent and adept.

The Gorsons in the Spanierman Gallery

Aaron Harry Gorson, 1872–1933

1. *"Furnace"*

Sabbath midnight marked the start
Of my first day in the mills, feeding the salts
Of my sweat to the face of the flames,

Learning the arts of the shovel
And the stubbornness of time.
Who knew the old industrial order

Was about to come ticking to its end,
Ushering in the seven years of famine
And all the Rust Belt ones after that?

Gorson never took the mills for granted,
Or the way that the open hearths
Seemed to alchemize light.

In his painting *Furnace,* the nova of molten metal
Is framed by an open door,
Transforming pigment into its ingot—

A midnight sun I stood before,
In heat as arid and solar, in front of the painting,
Back in that wind.

2. "Mills at Night"

If it weren't for the smokestacks above them
Those silhouettes could be foothills
Converging along the river,

Funneling the dark toward the open hearth
Dead-centered in their midst.
A painting almost equal parts water and sky.

Besides the black of the factory mass,
There's cerulean and cobalt and Prussian blue
Off-loaded from his brush,

The furnace on its spit of horizon
An impastoed scarlet dot
Within the pale yellow geyser of the smoke.

Everything vectored and balanced,
The corner of the barge in the foreground
Tethered to the corner of the pier.

Flecks of light, here and there,
Floating on the river.
Banks of clouds above them, scattered about.

Insomnia

Howard Johnson Motor Inn, 1992

Pittsburgh, 4 a.m., I wake in the hold
Of the neck-prickling hives of panic,
Alone in the dark of the city I grew up in,
And no closer, it would seem, to home.
Sleep, they say, is always the first casualty.
I'll be stranded here for hours, the sodium glow
Of the arc-lamps in their corridors below,
And in the room the light from the TV.
Night watch and night sweats. A steady state
Of blizzards that won't let up till dawn
When the reruns give way, the reedy psalms
Dissolve into static and a new day.
Clicking off the set I'll see my face, a day-moon,
Ghostly, near-transparent, loom upon the tube.

Moby-Dick

Leona Theater, Homestead, 1956

First the light-flooded curtains parting like the sea.
Then that rucksacked figure making his way
Among the trees and fountain spray
Of the cataract, diagonally down the screen,
When all at once from the darkness
The paused imperative comes: "Call me   Ishmael."
I'm still trying to account for the thrill
Of those syllables on a boy as clueless
As me. But even before Queequeg, the *Pequod,*
Or Ahab appears, before the stark masts fill
With St. Elmo's fire, the film with Pip's
Revelation that the whale was a great white god,
I'm hooked, just blocks above the sullen mills
That will in time become my whale ship.

Among Ruins

Waterfront Shopping Complex—
Former Homestead Works, U.S. Steel

1. *Smokestack, 160-Inch Mill*

Pillar, obelisk, mast.
It loomed beside the bridge
Since before I was born,
A minaret from which
They might have marked
The shifts. Steel-sheathed
And lined with brick.
20 feet wide at the base
They've imploded, a blow
Like a sledge, and then
The slow-motion buckle
And forward pitch—a last
Controlled blast, where
We'd dreamt of winds
Endless as the centuries,
The *dead calm of masonry*
Melville once traced in
The pyramids. *As long*
as earth endures, he wrote,
some vestige will remain.
Which is the way we'd
Thought about the mills:
Ruins like fabulous tombs.

"A last nail in the coffin
of something that died
15 years ago," a mill hunk
Complained. And Melville:
*no moss as in other ruins—
no grace of decay—no ivy—*

*2. Words Written for the Historical Marker Planned
for the 12,000-Ton Press*

Scrolled and monumental, 40 feet high,
It stands in the lot behind Lowe's
Like something Mayan, cleared from the vines,
The housing sheared away,
The forging division, and the press shop.

What's left are the shafts of the double ram,
The entablature massive as a headdress.
And those 17 feet of base—
A counterweight sunk beneath the blacktop.

Think of it: this out-compressed the planet
In pounds per square inch, water oceanic
Through the surge tanks and pumps.

Stele and relic. Tool and die.
And now these words to remember it by.

The Book of Generations Tucked among the Pages of the Family Bible

He was given a decorative plate showing
an Irish peasant scene.
                      —*Homestead Local News*

Inside the crumbling leather covers,
Among the kingdoms of the Word,
I rummage for that scissored clipping,
Wondering again about its plate—
The one in which Thomas Caddy,
My great-great-uncle, saw the world
He'd lost by coming to the States
Recast as a version of the pastoral.

*

On the shield of Achilles, gold burns
Through the rich tilled earth
Where plowmen turn at the ends
Of their furrows, so what makes
A peasant scene *Irish*—rows
Of potatoes like sprouting stones?
The dark curd cut from peat bogs
Larded with keepsakes of their own?

*

I know that nothing of Homestead
Was glazed upon that plate—
No slag pots or cloud-shot columns
Towering above the open hearths—
And guess that he arrived at longing
Unexpectedly, like the rest of us,
As if longitude meant the measure
Of such distances in the heart.

The Negro Leagues

1. At the Renaming Ceremony

July 12, 2002

A gift from our third-term mayor,
This change of names from *High Level*
To *Homestead Grays,* the bridge
To the same poor Rust Belt shore now hung
With plaques of fabric, a lamppost gallery
In which portraits have been draped—
Josh Gibson, Satchel Paige, Cool Papa Bell . . .
Plaques like battle standards, I almost wrote,
That stormed the color barrier, a story
Well known to everyone by now,
But not how victory also meant the death
Of the Negro Leagues, teams looted
For their best players, then left to make do,
Diminished as their communities.
Here at the beginning of a new century
The Grays are being trotted out again
To play a part in the town's rebranding,
The steel mills gone in which they got
Their start as the sandlot Blue Ribbons.
Straka's Restaurant is gone as well
Where the Grays' owner, Cumberland Posey
Bought rounds for the house, though
He wasn't allowed to drink there himself.
A friend of my father's, as far as things went,
The arcs of their lives just abutting.

I never guessed back then how much
The connection, tenuous as it might have
Seemed, would come to mean to me later,
As did the one to the battered earth
I'd watched them dump into the furnaces,
One shift after another in the mills.

2. *Keeping Score*

My father taught me how to keep a scorecard,
    The vestige of an affection

He'd had all his life, growing up in Homestead
    With the Grays. He'd fill his pages

With that crisp familiar script and save them—
    A way of replaying afternoons

When love was itself a kind of summer:
    "Late innings you could see your mother

Turning the color of their gloves." Back then
    Even the sandlot teams were terrific.

Players like Harold Tinker. Once, at the A-Field,
    He showed me the plaque

For Cumberland Posey, flanked by his dates.
    And once on our front porch,

Baited by a neighbor demanding to know
    If he wanted his son marrying

One of them, he stood his ground, who'd pulled
    For Robinson and Doby.

3. "The Homestead Grays"

Photograph by Teenie Harris, Pittsburgh Courier

Here in the photograph and past their prime
In 1942, they're posed in Forbes Field
In traditional rows, half the team kneeling,
The grandstand's struts and girders behind
Them like a maze of fire escapes.
Buoquet Street in the background softly lit.
And the white swabs of those uniforms—
Pale bolls that ghosted into the darkroom.
Years later, my father still read the newspaper
They'd graced. I loved to look at the comics:
Strips like negatives of the ones I knew,
First exposures to a world of Jim Crow
Robinson had played in, and sweet Ted Page,
To whom I was once related through marriage.

Donny

Memory's meager: that he was a member
Of the congregation, that he lived catty-corner
From the church and was related somehow
To a friend of mine or was a friend of the family.

I remember he'd once been a boxer,
A welterweight my father said took it on the chin,
Glass the word I remember, and his flat
Refracted nose. But why I was at his house

Having dinner one Sunday after Mass
I don't remember, only that my parents
Needed to be off somewhere together,
Attending to whatever it was that couldn't wait.

So much is tangent here—who knows what
Or whom, whose life is being sidetracked
Or running its course—so much absorbed
Into the ordinary where it's taken on faith.

A narrow, high-ceilinged dining room,
Bulbs in sconces, old discolored wallpaper
On which baskets of bouquets were hung,
And everyone doting upon me.

Why's memory so insistent on this fragment?
My parents must have claimed me
At the time arranged, the formal exchanges
Of debt and relief completed above my head.

Was I always welcome? I'm drawing a blank.
What remains are the hours I spent alone
In a parlor they kept Victorian with rubber trees
And ferns and overstuffed pieces of furniture.

While the household went about its rhythms
I watched whatever the windows had to offer,
Poked again through the comic-strips:
L'il Abner, Terry and the Pirates, Joe Palooka,

Which reminded me, of course, of Donny.
When I got home I was going to ask again
About that nose, how something could heal
And yet still be broken.

W. Eugene Smith: Three Photographs

1. *"The Dance of Flaming Coke," 1955*

Shielding his face, he looks at first
To be kneeling before the whirlwind,
His body distorted by the heat,

The heavy gouts of smoke erupting
From the oven he's clamped a lid on,
Like a manhole cover on a street.

Spraddled, backlit against the cirrus
Of light-riddled steam, he's all alone,
At least in the photo, caught between

The not-quite-parallel set of rails
Smith's highlighted with ferrocyanide,
Bright lines vanishing diagonally

Through the sulfurs of that Tophet.
They've been seamed into the floor
As if from some cleaner geometry—

Another instance of his "equilibriums,"
The contrasts he sought to balance,
Object and subject, man and machine.

2. *"Man Lost in a Maze of Railroad Tracks," 1955*

Even as small and blurred and pale
As pictured here, he's still central,

Slotted by the spidery tracks
Directing him away from us, back

Among the branchings of that maze.
Pairs of flat symmetrical sprays—

They're all he has to go by,
Lost in darkness, gauging his stride.

Man's a moth, the photograph says,
And everything around him's a web.

3. *"Rails, Homestead Works, U.S. Steel,
Monongahela River," 1955*

The itemizing title spells everything out
Except for the fact that it's twilight and the rails
Gleam like mercury poured into grooves
Ribboning the width of the switching yard.
On one side, a riverbank black as night.
On the other, the solid shadow of a hill.
That sliver of river confined to the right-
Hand corner means he's on the Rankin Bridge,
Staring into the sun. Viewed from there
The mills form a first faint horizon, the ridge
Above them a strip of dusk just slightly grayer
Than the sky, off-white with particulates.
The whole of the photo capped by the dark
Deckled edge of smoke spreading from the flues.

"Beauties of the Common Tool"

Photographs by Walker Evans, Fortune, *July 1955*

Pliers, tin snips, crescent wrench . . .
He's centered each one in the field

Of his undivided attention,
Where it seems to float suspended

In a world of mists, inviting the hand
To test its heft and balance,

The eye to admire the way he's lit
The sleek and sculptural metal—

That graphite shimmer
That's equal parts hardware and art.

After all, there is no part of them
Which does not fit perfectly

With whatever task they've been set.
Including the photographs'

Where light's been made to coalesce
In each dense, mist-bound shape,

Forged steel alluring as a magnet,
The planet of its page.

Industrial Pittsburgh: Works on Paper

1. Whistler on the Smithfield Street Bridge

Winter twilight, the last flights of pigeons
Wheeling home above the river,
Wisps of cirrus like scratches in glass.
Again tonight the great buildings have turned
Transparent, their weightless sides
The same gray as the sky—an equilibrium
He knows will soon give way to the darkness
Massing in their shapes, to mill smoke
And gas lamps erasing the terraced stars.
But for now, from the bow of the bridge,
Scumblings of mist on the river,
Pittsburgh looks celestial, hovering in midair,
The way water does in the distance
Above whatever mirror might cast it there.

2. Turner in Homestead

Unmistakable—the way the landscape,
Which is light on water, becomes the sky
And Homestead the river-hemmed Venice
He's painted keelmen floating coal to at night,
The red flecks of their deck lamps
Daubed within the loose notational haze.
Those flat black shadows are steel mills,
Vast as the Doge's Palace, stretching back
Along the floodplain. Come daylight
He'll render their smoke as drifting plumes

Low on the watery horizon, stoked ovens
Howling in a blizzard of pastels . . .
It's there in his sketches, that pairing of light
With coal fires burning on the river at night.

3. *Piranesi Discovers Open Hearth #5*

Conte crayons and sketchpads, their pages
Packed with the soot-black shadows
Cast by catwalks, chimneys, scaffolds—
All in that welter of piled-up perspectives
We've come to recognize as his: a space
Both cavernous and congested. It's as though
Here in the mills he's entered one of his own
Imaginary prisons, their fantastic maze
Of chambers no less starved for light.
Hoist chains and rafters. The train tracks
And carriages of the overhead cranes, slabs
Stacked by them to a tenement height.
Yet in here everything is *under,* a necropolis
Right from his dreams. He can't get over it.

Dreiser First Glimpses *Sister Carrie* in the Stacks of the Carnegie Library

Pittsburgh, 1893

Barely weeks at his dream job, working
A beat, and he's holed up in the library,
Snug inside an alcove on a rainy afternoon,
Light mullioned in the lead-glass windows.

All month he's been burrowing his way
Through Balzac: *Père Goriot* and *Cousin Pons*,
The Great Man of the Provinces . . .
"Open pictures of self-indulgence and vice,"

Like ones he's found spread all around him—
Red-light districts the size of wards,
Gaming houses and pool halls
Where aldermen idle on the public dime.

"We don't touch on labor conditions,"
He'd been warned the first day at the paper,
Or "scandals in high life," or "the rich
and religious in a derogatory sense."

But here in Balzac's teeming chapters
He's glimpsed a mode of approach
Whose manner he might follow
Into every corner of the human moil.

"To go to the city," he'd once proclaimed,
"is the changeless desire of the mind."
Now that he's done so he's come to believe
That all such desires are "chemic,"

Part of the tangle of circumstance
And chance, the very contagion of *things*
Among which he'll soon loose Carrie Meeber,
The vague entourage of her dreams.

Making Pittsburgh Stogies

Lewis Hine, 1909

"Multiple originals," they'd be called
As prints or photos. "Mass-produced," if cast
In the mold behind her or emptied
From the press where the molds get stacked.
If this weren't a factory, her motions
Carpal tunnel, you might speak more of craft.
After all, she's bunched them leaf by leaf,
Though they look like sticks of graphite
Or cartridges greased in heaps. In fact,
They look like their name suggests, piece-rate
And dime-a-dozen, assembled by rote if not
By line, trimmed and rolled and wrapped.
She's there in profile, chignon at her neck,
Cigars piling up like hours, one to the next.

Ahmad Jamal Playing the Piano at the Kay Boys' Club, ca. 1945

Charles "Teenie" Harris

He's all spruced up and beaming
In front of the battered upright,
A trumpet case beneath him
So he can more easily reach the keys.
The Mozart of Apple Avenue,
He's now halfway through his teens
And that many years again
From his fabled gig at the Pershing.
A few sheets of music lie open
On the rack, the piano's hammers
Showing where the inlaid panel
Should be: crammed-together notes
He'll find a way to space within
His meticulous, shifting rhythms.
There's a "this better be good" look
On the face of the man standing
Canted against the wall behind him—
An early critic perhaps of the style
Dismissed by some as *cocktail*,
Though Miles was always taken
With the intelligence of its phrasing.
"Poinciana," most famously,
And "But Not for Me," the megahit
He'd refuse to play for years,
Suffering his version of early success.
To have had all of that packed

And waiting, right from the start!
Who's had a bigger send off?
"Pittsburgh meant everything to me
and it still does," he would say
Decades later. In the photograph,
The bentwood back of his chair
Is as elegantly scrolled as a clef.

The Piano

Silent, it was just another piece of furniture

In my aunt's living room, its black gloss
Upright and dusted in turn, and the bench

In which sheet music was stashed away,
Hinged under wraps like the keyboard.

A world my boredom barely disturbed,

Sending a few stray notes into the room,
The pedals doing nothing, it seemed,

Whether I floored them or not. What tunes
Would I have been noodling anyway

Back in 1955, if I'd even known how—

"Misty" perhaps? Or "Erroll's Theme"?
My father's Methodist half-sister

Would have allowed neither to disturb
The waters of the river Jordan

Stoppered in that jar on top of her TV.

Whatever songs she pounded out for me
Were hymnal, her strict fingers marching

Off to war. Even "Be Thou My Vision,"
Which I couldn't listen to for years,

Till Van Morrison roused it like a song

You might hear in a pub. Spiritus and spirits.
She'd hardly have approved of that.

Plodding, plagal, in service to their words,
The tunes were mostly cupboard bare.

It seemed she knew them all by heart.

Jobs Report

i.

Magee-Womens Hospital, the days
I worked maintenance, clearing out
The old wards and wooden shelves
Where files had once been stored,
Giving myself over at the end of each
To the rain of traffic, the lurching
Progress of the bus, lulled by August
And the engine's steady hum.
I'd fall asleep while the aisle filled up
With its silent sway of passengers,
At the end of another workday
They'd spent watching the clock,
Wishing it were time to punch-out.
Years will have to pass before
It dawns on me that this is the answer
To their wish, and that by morning
It will hardly seem to matter,
Having been delivered out of labor
For such a paltry time. Diesel mists
Trailing us to the High Level Bridge,
Where the great banks of river light
Would wake me, I'd begin dreaming
Of the evening ahead—gleaming cars
And the first girls on the sidewalks,
Parading beneath the luxury
Of the summer trees. And if work
Meant days given over to drudgery
And sweat, I was young and every
Other week brought its paycheck.

ii.

All that August we hauled desks
Down from the attic of the nurses' dorm,
Surrounded by the rustle of uniforms,
The buss of nylons as they rushed by,
Sweet-smelling and candy-striped.
We stacked the desks in storage
Beside the banged-up beds and bureaus
From the hospital's remodeled wards,
And stretched our work-breaks out
Up there, lolling among the mattresses.
High in the heaven of that room
We blustered the mysteries, regaling
Each other with stories about nurses,
The tropic heat of divorcees. Bert,
The first dirty old man I'd met for real,
Would cackle about getting it up.
Geno, his voice fragrant with tobacco,
Would remember nights in Bloomfield,
The summers when he was young.
Women like flowering plums!
Although no one ever said as much,
Sex was clearly a sacrament, the body
Anointed with its oils, saturated with
A passion that heaved it clear of time.
Sprawled on top of a mattress
Where love's cries had never passed,
I closed my eyes and conjured up
The dusky blossoms of the body,
Its rosettes and figlike flesh, pigments
As lurid as the Sacred Heart's
Bedded in petals of flame. Then Bert
Made that crack about black cherries,
Geno pressed the wafer-sized packet
Into my palm and pronounced me
Ready for work. So I made my way

Back to the attic, its stash of desks,
But this time pocketing that Trojan,
My token of admission, they'd joked.

The Dinner Pail

Photo courtesy of Steve Simko

Less lunchbox than mess kit,
What with that fitted lid

And handle, the canister set inside it,
Cap threaded tight—

All got toted off to work in the mills,
The pail as much a staple

As the bread and tea and leftover meats:
Meals unpacked like job lots.

At the end of the shift
It went back on the shelf

Till the next day, a soon-to-be vestige
Of the Industrial Age.

Catalogued here,
The metal's sheen is gelatin silver,

Its tin stamped and banded
Like a galvanized can.

I brown-bagged my meals,
Years later, to the 100-inch mill,

Though there were days when
My hours by the ovens

Flayed me with such heat
I wondered how anyone could eat.

Historical Portraits

1. John McClure

Chinese lanterns on the mansion lawns: summer,
1851, McClure Street climbing above the river

To where the old Amity Homestead ends.
Cow's Hill, as it was known back then—

Platty and undeveloped—when the McClures sold
Off acres to their own company,
                              to then unload

As single lots, turning a tidy profit.
"Entrepreneurs," we'd say, using the current argot.

Take old John.
              The first of that family's scions,
He'd traded with both British and Indians,

Increasing the fortune he'd put into land
To retire on as a "country gentleman."

Politics was the next prestige,
Father an ardent Federalist, the son a prominent Whig.

2. *Philander C. Knox*

Think Louis Calhern, say at the beginning
Of *The Asphalt Jungle,* pinstriped, pulling the strings.

Carnegie's colluding attorney,
He'd charged the Homestead strikers with conspiracy,

Having himself helped bilk the city
In a land deal—
              the neat piece of jobbery

That expanded both his fortunes and the mills.
Afterwards, he was moved to Justice: the Sleepy Phil

Who nodded while the Trusts grew up, and State,
Where he gave us Dollar Diplomacy and United Fruit.

"The best lawyer I have ever had for our interests,"
Wrote Frick.
        A late collusion locked Honduras

Within the American sphere, banana plantations
Run by men thuggish as the Pinkertons.

Newspaper Days: Dreiser in Pittsburgh, 1893–1894

> Dreiser discarded his "romantic" rural perspective:
> "I had seen Pittsburgh!"
> —David E. Shi, *Facing Facts*

Chapter LIX

"What a city for a realist," he crowed,
Come by train past the muddy yellow lanes
And grimy houses of the mining towns,
The soot-faced miners with their oil-and-tow
Tin lamps, the babushka-clad women
Hanging clothes. All under the gaze
Of the Coal & Iron police—armed goons
On horseback. And though he'd scoffed
At editorials chorused in Carnegie's defense
When the union was broken in Homestead,
He still wants to work for a newspaper
And alights with his letter of reference
At the foot of the Smithfield Street Bridge.
Streetcars and wagons. Steamboats
Like threshers chopping their swaths.
And along the factory shore before him,
Tongues of fire licking the air,
Ten, twelve feet above the blow stacks,
And that sound he'll liken to anvils
Being pounded underground. Transfixed,
By the time he seeks lodgings in the smoke-
Stained city, the gas lamps are being lit.

Chapter LX

The next morning he's up and devouring
The local papers, counting the number
Of columns lavished across each society page,
The small-print précis of the injuries
Suffered most recently in the mills. Days before
The *Dispatch* hires him, he's already taken
A trolley out among the neighborhoods,
The Incline to the top of Mt. Washington,
Vantaging a city—molten spires,
Rivers like flowing lava—that even Rome
Won't match. But then here he's the cub
Reporter. Pigeons bright as swallows flock
His skies, and nights with their glistering stars.
It's not all heaven, the city editor warns him:
"There's nothing to be said about the rich.
The big steel men here just about own
this place." As if he hadn't figured that much
Out by himself, strolling one afternoon
In Millionaire's Row where the lawns alone
Are baronial and the streets get washed
Like the private drives, the horse-drawn cabs,
Liveried, clattering across the Belgian block.

Chapter LXI

He'll find unpaved streets in Homestead
A year and a half after the strike,
The clapboard houses grown sullen and dark.
Ore yards and open hearths, cigar cars
Smoldering on the Hot Metal Bridge.
And at shift's end, streaming out, the men
With their empty tin pails, sunlight
Slanting through burnished clouds of dust.
Come summer he'll be there among them,
Taking notes: ovens like in Deuteronomy
Where the foundations of the mountains
Have been set on fire, puddlers keeping
Pig iron at a boil, slag skimmed off
Through the cinder notches. None of which
Makes it into the pages of the *Dispatch*.
The best he can manage, months he's here,
Is slip a few tenements into his account
Of a rainstorm slaking the city, dissolving
The bridge-heads and buildings in fog,
Sluicing the mud-strewn gutters—as if
It were all just so much local color
And not the profit of the earth spilling off.

IV

Looking through the Entries in an Old Pocket Notebook

Then there's this—the gist of a sentence
Written down from memory
And left as if pressed between pages:

fixing the present in the districts of the past . . .

Something to do with photography perhaps,
The image in its fixative bath?

It's got me thinking about Eugène Atget
In his dawn-drenched city,
Out prowling the cul-de-sacs,

The vignette doorways and storefronts
Flashed on dry plate negatives
Like the ghostly held breaths of their glass.

The way he could have done in Pittsburgh,
Setting up those long exposures
In the long-gone Jenkins Arcade,

Or across the street from Kaufmann's clock
Where the dead still arrange to meet—

Dissolving figures in the solvents of light—

The time above them focal and frozen,
The shadows all silver nitrate.

Children Going Home from School to New Raw Suburbs (1952): Photograph by Clyde Hare

i.

The block-shaped houses sit squarely
On their lots, back from the road

That winds at a bias, gradually up
The slope, the level late-day shadows

Runged across each insular lawn.
No sidewalks or porches,

No vestiges of the old forests left.
A recent people, at odds with time.

ii.

Blinkered in line with the light,
The houses might have just emerged

From the ground—*the grassie Clods
now Calv'd*—the road between them

Gleaming, a brushed-nickel strip
Upon which schoolchildren scatter,

Darkness covering the foreground,
Settling on the crest of the hill.

iii.

How enormous the world is then,
Darkness threaded by a vein of light,

The children halfway home
Suspended on its translucence,

Emptiness surrounding the houses,
Phone poles spaced in place of trees.

How enormous the terraced shadows
Dividing what's left of the light.

iv.

In Hare's photo *Federal Street*, 1951
The houses—two-story, residential

Above the first-floor shops—
Are chock-a-block and Victorian,

Topped with chimney pots.
Parked cars, traffic, trolley tracks.

A bric-a-brac of sunlight and shadow,
The late-day houses closing ranks.

Childhood

Pittsburgh, winter, the mid-nineteen-fifties,
Drifts of snow pitted with cinders
And rock-salt, and all of it, in memory,
Gray as our old Chevy, pulled hastily over
To the side of the road, all of it gray as the billboard
(Some down-payment dream) in front of which
I've just been sick to my stomach.
We're on our way to visit my father again,
Locked up in the ward of the asylum
Because the world which is all in his head
Has to be flashed from its circuits like bits of the past.
I remember the lattice at the billboard's base,
The trash and passing traffic. A gray world,
Like my father's, where I found myself lost.

Double Shot

i.

My father in his cups, this his recitation—
Barney Bigard, Jimmy Yancey, Zutty Singleton—

Names like the ones of fabled cities
He loved visiting—*Zoot Sims* and *Kid Ory*—

Their lingua franca a speaking in tongues,
The raptures of scat. But *Monk*

I stumbled upon on my own one week
On the cover of *Time* magazine,

And after that in the record bins
Where I found him featured in profile again,

The swirling smoke from his cigarette
The atmosphere in which he'd been set,

Goateed and hatted, face lifted at a slant
Amid shifting notes, displaced accents.

ii.

That the photograph was one of Gene Smith's
I wouldn't have even noticed

Or known enough to care.
That would take me years. Years more

To hear the story of his knocking a hole
Clear through the wall in his studio

So he could listen to them playing next door,
Augmenting their intricate chords.

In his "jazz loft project" there's a shot
Of the building in staggered silhouettes,

Flat as the backdrop in a play,
Windows whose drama's repeatedly staged.

He'd be up there nights, working alone,
The one wall wailing in that Jericho.

View of Toledo

after El Greco

My eyes the two burnt holes in the blanket,
They'd tease, having awakened me

When it was time to go, leaving my aunt's
For the drive back home

Past the shadowy hulks of factories,
The trowel-shaped city that rose into the night.

Beacons on the skyscrapers hovered,
The river's black mirror jeweled with their lights.

I'd watch for the blast furnaces at J&L,
Towering above the cloud-cover smoke,

For slag to spill like a meteor shower
Down its dark invisible hills.

Watch for the lit exotic crosses to appear
On the domes of the Orthodox Church.

The sign for Homestead floated overhead,
And then a sky as wide as the river valley

Where we crossed over water
And passed between the rooftops of U.S. Steel—

The casting sheds I would enter in turn,
Nights like fiery machinery,

Working in the darkness in a world of flame,
Ladles the Dippers above me.

Lunar Grammars

A blood-orange moon, huge and lucent,
Hanging above the horizon at the distant end
Of the parking lots. Hunter and Harvest,
      Pitted as if with rust.

On the graveyard shift it was bone-white
Or vellum, inching along, slow as the hands
Of a clock. It came up alongside the river—
      Full or half or quartered—

And in the mornings faded out. Or stayed
In the sky all day like the lifted dust
Of a fingerprint, the boss of a watermark.
      New, it was part of the dark.

We had fire from the ovens, from the stars,
The humming machinery of the heavens
They'd invented back in the Age of Steam,
      The great gears gleaming.

The moon was goddess somewhere else,
And planter's companion, synodic, a presider
Over tides. Nature was somewhere else,
      Or converted into resource,

The river a place to run off wastes, carp
You couldn't eat, the fires out on the waters
Something you shouldn't swim through,
      Though we did, the moon

Those nights as close as you could get
To shining, slipping beneath the surface,
Then rising from the river, shedding light.
    The same river twice,

I think, walking beside it as though tracking
That shine. The same fluvial moon—
First bone, then blood—disking the sky,
        Locative, then ablative, in time.

On Foot

1. *Cleats*

The time of cobblers. The craze was cleats—
Small, tack-hammered crescents
I remember mostly on motorcycle boots,

The way they threw off showers of sparks,
Part of the pageantry of Harleys
And black leather jackets studded with stars.

Still shy of my teens, they reminded me
Of the heavy clink of spurs
Scored like music for the westerns on TV.

All of which is why I wound up in that shop
In my stocking feet, breathing the scents
Of neatsfoot oil and polish. Shod,

I hit the sidewalk, eager to strike
The steel-heeled notes I'd been dreaming
Would play percussion to my strides.

A staccato I couldn't get loud enough,
Hard as I might kick, who hadn't gone a block
Before I'd scraped the first one off.

It looked like something fallen from a nest—
Flat and mangled, the brads of the legs—
Something I'd now think of, every other step.

2. *Prosthetic*

Basic at best, the state of the art back then
For artificial limbs like the one my friend's
Mill-hunk father left lying about the house.

He'd find it from time to time, beside the couch
Or stashed away in the closet,
A spare part that was always in stock.

It stood its ground, regardless, replete with shoe
And sock—a wooden leg made of plastic,
The skin tinted like a mannequin's.

Hinged, hefty, a contraption of straps,
We imagined the blows it could deliver,
The kicks that shin could easily deflect.

Anything's a toy in the hands of boys
Wearing the novelty off. Every morning
Imagine having to strap on what you've lost.

3. *The Atomic Age*

The bones of my feet in the X-ray machine
At Thom McAn's—a cache of backlit fossils
In the invisible clasp of those shoes.

The Art of Memory

i.

Because it's memory, I see myself in long-shot,
Halfway up the chain-link fencing
At the back of the yard. Before me is orchard,
The cloud-white blossoms of the beckoning world.
Not yet three years old, my feet fit perfectly
Into the mesh of diamonds I'm clutching
A handful at a time, almost to the rail on top—
The line of that horizon eye-level with the sky.

ii.

Memory, in whose distances were glimpsed
The first sketchy inklings of perspective.

iii.

"Get down from there before you kill yourself!"
My frantic aunt shouting from a window
In the kitchen, her small face framed
Above my shoulder when I crane for a look.

iv.

Figures fanning from their vanishing points,
Recessional along the sightlines.

v.

This is the house that memory's kept for me,
With its pocket doors and wood floors
And rooms set perimeter to the stairwell.
Where my place at the table is beside my aunt
After my Uncle Arch's burial, amazed
To find them all chattering away as usual
When the world had just come to an end.
I'd been in bed all week with a fever.
Alone, I remember, as if stranded at his grave.

vi.

Perspicere, as the light passes through,
As the clear light strikes the eye.

vii.

Memory being the backscatter.

Envoy: *University Center Mural* (1995–1996), Carnegie Mellon University

The jostled precincts, their cram and heave,
Panoramic from the railing of the mezzanine,

Clouds scudding in flotilla above the rooftops
And the cumulus tops of the trees.

Bridges and beltways. Our river-locked city
In oxidized lines, sooted chiaroscuros,

The sunset-side of houses a fire on the scale
Of the great mills burning everywhere . . .

All of it salvaged from the rubble and dust
Like the dolphins on the walls at Knossos.

NOTES

"100-Inch Mill, Special Plate Finishing Facility": Lightnin' Hopkins's "Moon Rise Blues" can be found on *The Complete Aladdin Recordings* (EMI Records, 1991). Blues aficionados will notice I've taken liberties with the lyrics.

"Among Ruins": The italicized lines are from Herman Melville's *Journal up the Straits*.

"Historical Portraits": The phrase "platty and undeveloped" is from William Serrin's book *Homestead: The Glory and Tragedy of an American Steel Town* (Times Books, 1992).

"*Newspaper Days*: Dreiser in Pittsburgh, 1893–1894": The title comes in part from Theodore Dreiser's *A Book about Myself* (Fawcett, 1965).

"*Children Going Home from School to New Raw Suburbs* (1952): Photograph by Clyde Hare": The italicized lines in part two come from book 7 of John Milton's *Paradise Lost*.

ROBERT GIBB

was born in the steel town of Homestead, Pennsylvania.
He is the author of eleven books of poetry,
including *The Origins of Evening*, which was a National Poetry
Series winner. He has received numerous awards,
including two National Endowment for the Arts grants,
seven Pennsylvania Council on the Arts grants,
a Best American Poetry Prize, a Pushcart Prize,
and The Marsh Hawk Poetry Prize, among others.
He lives on New Homestead Hill
above the Monongahela River.

www.ingramcontent.com/pod-product-compliance
Lightning Source LLC
Chambersburg PA
CBHW062118080426
42734CB00012B/2908